Good words for *Memories L[*
Gerald

MW00452030

MEMORIES LOOKING THROUGH A SC[[...rald Bigelow is a
collection of poems that are a quiet protest against racism, a tribute to loved ones, a
snapshot of communities, a history of time and place, an exploration of spirituality,
and ultimately, the inevitability of aging. Read them for the beauty of language and
lines that shatter you like from "Must" where a circus parade goes through town and
"lions reach out/paw the air/create a fearful silence." Read them for their exploration
of race. In "It No Longer Matters," Bigelow explores how "[y]our 1950s and my 1950s
were not the same." And finally, read his poems for his astute musings on the realties
of growing older. In "The World is Getting Old," Bigelow observes his own aging
noting that, "[in the mirror] I look and see lines and creases/ must be some kind of
flaw in the glass."

-Laura Moe, author of *Breakfast with Neruda*, named one of NYPL's Best Books for
Teens 2016, and Top Shelf VOYA 2016, WA State Book Award Finalist 2018

With wry wit and deep wisdom, poet Gerald Bigelow comments on life in all its beauty
and despair, as seen through the filter of time.

-Judith Works, author of *Coins in the Fountain: A Memoir of Rome*

Gerald Bigelow 's poetry opens the door to share his memories, a view of life, as well as
social and cultural identity across his decades as a sensitive observer of the world
around him.

-Paddy Eger, award-winning YA author of *84 Ribbons*, *When the Music Stops*, and
Letters to Follow, and *Tasman*

Gerald Bigelow's poetry collection *Memories Looking Through a Screen Door* includes
reflections on his life experiences and on aspects of the human condition. He writes
with curiosity and conviction, of countries and borders, small moments of daily life,
and tolerance and prejudice, the journey from childhood toward old age. With a spirit
sometimes heavy, sometimes light, Bigelow opens his heart. You will find poetry here
that touches you and prompts reflection on your own life, whether or not you've ever
looked through a screen door.

-Joanne Bradury-Peterson, contributing author to *Writing in Place* and well-known
columnist for *the Edmonds Beacon*

While books take many pages to transport readers into other worlds, gifted poet Gerald
Bigelow skillfully uses a few succinct words to usher us into the depths of his life's
experiences. Whether a whimsical lyric on nature or a heart-wrenching history of
injustice, Gerald's indomitable spirit, the spark that gives him life, persists and leaves the
reader transformed.

- Kizzie Elizabeth Jones, M. Div., BCC, and author of the *Tall Tales* children's books

Gerald Bigelow has written not simply a book of poetry but a book of wisdom. He writes of life, a collective humanity that pulls at reader's heartstrings, weaving them into the tapestry of humankind. This book of perception, filtered through the prism of color, and stained by witnessing time, is a voice--food to a hungry horde--it begs to share poignant memories with its peers and to be a sage witness to a younger generation. These poems have the uncanny power of illuminating the poet's personal journey as a black man, while recounting both history and life at the same time.

-Mindy Halleck, award-winning fiction author, motivational speaker, writing instructor, and winner of 2015 Return to Sender Reader's Choice Award

Memories Looking Through a Screen Door

Gerald M. Bigelow

Poet and Author: Gerald M. Bigelow

Designed by Tracy Long Graphic Design LLC and set in Apple Chancery and Adobe Caslon Pro typefaces.

Cover Photography: Cheryl Armstrong

Back Cover Photography: James Backstrom

Pg. 39 Photography: Vivian Murphy

All additional photography downloaded from pexels.com

Acknowledgments

Kizzie Jones,my friend, thank you for your guidance and support regarding the book release celebration process.
You are truly a source of support and encouragement.

Sherrie Bigelow, Hon, thank you for your encouragement and willingness to review and read my poems out loud, thus giving voice to my words.

Jared Bigelow, Son, as a fellow writer, your words, critiques and opinions matter, thus helping to improve the quality of my work.

Judith Works, my friend, your continuous leadership within the writing community has helped to increase the respect for the value of the literary arts within the Edmonds Arts community at large.

Vance Daddi, my friend and brother, your skills as a fellow writer and philosopher have been the constant voice over 50 plus years, challenging me to speak without fear.

Elyse Coulson, my friend and sister, your incredible talents and spirituality, helps to keep me focused on the beauty and good that exists in this World.

Tracy Long, thank you for possessing the skills, talent and patience for making the success of this project possible.

Jim Backstrom, thank you for your friendship and for being my go-to poetry editor. Your scholarly presence and the quality of your poetry has served as the foundation for the continued success of our EPIC sponsored poetry group.

Table of Contents

Chez Moi (Home and Neighborhood)

When Ever I Think of Snow — 2

I Miss my Cousin Sylvia — 3

Blowing up Tony — 4

Just Another Day in the Neighborhood — 6

No One Ever Tells You — 8

Down the Road — 10

They Came in Droves — 11

Time Knows — 12

Not Knowing — 13

Who was that Masked Man? — 13

Auntie Grace's Afghan — 14

Conversations at Cafe Du Monde — 15

Envy — 16

Uncle Blue — 18

Edmonds in the Dead of Winter — 20

The City at 4:04 am — 21

Winter Sledding on my Hill — 22

Must — 23

Valentine (The Search) — 24

A Gathering around the Family Piano — 26

Snohomish Valley Autumn
(Why I love this town) — 28

Remembering My Grandfather — 30

Sun Sets in the Southwest

Reasonable Expectations? (Sarcasm) — 32

Reasonable Expectations Revisited — 33

I Love the Desert but I can't Stand the Heat — 34

Men who put the "Boy" in Cowboy — 35

El Dormido Con Tres Perros
(The Sleeping Man with 3 Dogs) — 36

Because you are Family — 38

Too Hot to Handle

Liberated Women   40

The Plight of Old Black Women   41

Why Don't You Get it?   42

Actions that Bring Men to Tears   43

Stockholm Summer   44

St. Louis Twister (1988)   45

Metamorphosis   46

Why (Racism)

The Cost of Doing Business   48

It No Longer Matters   50

We Must Really Be Important   51

The County Line   51

Travel   52

That's What They Expect   54

Eyes on Nature

Song of Green Woods   56

Drifting   57

Spring Under the Cover of Night   57

Fall Colors   58

Observations   59

Winter Knocks   60

The Edmonds' Overnight Rain   60

Reflections   61

Making Your Presence Known   62

Fall Collection   62

The Mist   63

Spring (Predictability of Butterflies and Bumble Bees)   63

Day Dream   64

Oars and Sails

A Gentle Wind 66

The Lighthouse 66

The Keys 67

Amsterdam Dream 68

The Voice of the Seagull 70

There She Blows 71

Tall Ships Lost (Camden Harbor) 72

Crossing the bay 73

The Philosopher's Moment

I Believe 76

The Big Picture 76

Layers of Life 76

I Know You 77

Contrasting The Blue Moon 77

The World is Getting Old 78

My Cat 78

What Would You Say to God 79

Paradox Betrayal 80

Tapping on Cobblestones 81

Cutting Firewood 82

Living on the Edge 83

City Of Ascending Spires (Seattle) 84

Fragments and Phrases 84

Dexter Gordon 85

Perhaps 86

Comfort 86

Gazing at the Cascades 87

Stagnation 87

A Courtyard View of Spring 88

Electra 89

Chez Moi
(Home and Neighborhood)

When Ever I Think of Snow

Whenever I think of snow
I think of days before frost-free freezers

quaint back porches
with wringer-type washing machines

fuse boxes high on the clap board wall
neatly tucked away in the comer
out of reach

a flickering clear light bulb
suspended from the ceiling by a black cloth clad wire

whenever I think of snow
I think of a fireplace in the dining room
stoked by wood and coal

or a pot belly stove in the kitchen,
wood smoke mingling with the smells of, Gumbo, Mustard
Greens and Hot Water Cornbread,
making this the perfect gathering place

a meat locker -cold service porch bathroom
designed to discourage those who liked to linger

a hot brick, the electric blanket of the day,
heated in the fireplace
nestled in an old cotton towel
skillfully tucked under the covers at the foot of the bed

whenever I think of snow
I think of a saloon-like atmosphere and colorful language
unselfishly provided by cigar smoking favorite Uncles,

face powder stained shirts and exotic fragrances
resulting from hugging matronly, affection starved Aunts,

the rousing musical reverberations
emanating from the familiar patois of everyone talking at once

the endless clamor of spirited games of Bourée and Dominos

at day's end

full stomachs and empty bottles come to mind
whenever I think of snow.

I Miss my Cousin Sylvia

I miss my cousin Sylvia:

her image emblazoned upon my mind,
a permanent fixture astride the back of a maroon
1948 Indian Motorcycle,
forever an outlaw,
irascible, yet loveable,
an unrivaled memory,
her full face, cafe au lait complexion,
reddish brown hair trailing in the wind,
I can still see her stopping by, often on a sweltering summer afternoons,
strutting confidently across the lawn, pausing to wave at me,
giggling while stooping to get a drink of water from the faucet in our front yard,
deceptive and bold,
I can still remember that shamelessly, she would use me, her 7 year old cousin,
to pass the obligatory measure of respect due my Grandparents,
it was evident that she held in high regard the old ways of our Creole of Color Culture,
however, she could not abide the corset-like constrictions governing behavior,
not meeting Cousin Sylvia face to face suited my Grandparents just fine,
people said that my Cousin Sylvia had a way of courting disaster,
somehow, she always had a way of dealing with and being in control of the relationship,
if a cat had 9 lives, you can bet he borrowed 7 of them from Cousin Sylvia,

I can only hope,
that somewhere there is a cantankerous old woman,
sitting with a smug smile on her face,
reminiscing about:
the freedom she stole from life,
her triumphs over death and addiction,
and her battles with Love and Lust,
if our paths ever cross,
I hope that she has fond memories of me,
and that she knows,
I miss my cousin Sylvia,
Forever an outlaw,
Irascible, yet lovable.

Blowing up Tony

Adorned by skin the color of a perfect roux,
my cousin Tony's wife stood out in a crowd,
and was indeed a sight to behold,

she had refined features, framed by wavy black hair,
hair that fell about her neck and shoulders in a
manner reminiscent of the Jet Bead necklaces worn
by women of my Grandmother's generation,

a half-shade darker than his wife Joan,
Tony's striking features and curly hair gave him a
sophisticated air of confidence,

quiet and contemplative, a man of few words,
you could sit all night in a room with Tony and he
might utter ten words,
at other times even less,

he and his wife Joan were young and struggled to
make their way through the morass of culture and
tradition that defined New Orleans of the 1950s,

short on cash and long on dreams, they were forced
to come to my Grandparents to ask for a loan,
the money they sought was hard earned and
tightly held,

after enduring a stern lecture from my Grandparents covering
all topics known to mankind, including
"the meaning of life"
my Grandmother retrieved the money from a secure
hiding place and placed a nondescript envelope in Tony's hand,

a slight but well orchestrated nod of the head from
my Grandfather gave Tony and Joan permission to depart,

after a few farewells and a repeated round of "thank
yous," Tony and Joan returned to their car that was
conveniently parked across the street by the laundry,

on that Fall evening, the air was punctuated by a slight chill,
there was a noticeable uneasiness present in the mist
and fog that came off of the river,
an unanticipated flash, a deafening boom and flames,
sent my Grandfather and Uncle reaching for their
guns while scrambling to get to the front door,

I can vaguely remember the old folks saying that
Tony ran with the wrong crowd,

a tan and white ambulance came from the Orleans
Parish Colored-Charity Hospital,
and matter-of-factually removed Tony and Joan from the
scene,

the car burned until the fire went out,
then a tow truck came and routinely hauled the wreckage away,

do you think the Police came and conducted a
big investigation?

my Grandfather and Uncle who pulled Tony and
Joan from the fire, rarely spoke about what happened,

Tony's burns were superficial but his scars were deep
and lasting,

the blast and fire showed mercy to Joan, respectfully
sparing her face,

her arm severely burned and permanently scarred
became a constant reminder of the rules of the game,

ironically, while my Grandparents were trying to
ease the hardships in Tony's life,
someone was busy trying to take his life,

there were no tears or gnashing of teeth over what
had occurred,

frankly, we all knew that Tony ran with the wrong crowd,

as Autumn became Winter something changed
between the coming and going,

Tony changed and so did his friends!

at our place there were only infrequent whispers
among the men-folk about what happened,

why they tried to blow up Tony,
we may never know,

the whole event was like watching a "B" grade movie,
only this time we had front row seats, leaving our
customary seats in the balcony reserved for those
who tried to blow up Tony.

Just Another Day in the Neighborhood

The houses closest to the river were on the edge of town,
but at the heart of our community,
and foremost in my mind,

we rarely went to town,
preferring the solace of familiar surroundings,

in our neighborhood The Shell Oil Refinery dominated the landscape;
controlled politics and the economy,

it was the underpinning of our existence,
we never thought about health or safety issues,
neither did "They,"

as kids we were fascinated by the enormous rubber tree,
strategically placed at the refinery's entrance,
welcoming customers and visiting dignitaries,

to us, the tree was an exotic symbol of corporate benevolence,

on that day when the refinery caught on fire,
no one became alarmed,

not even when noxious fumes and smoke (as thick as
winter fog on Bayou La Fourche), obscured the horizon and
hid even the closest neighbors from each other,

we all stayed put,
no evacuation warning,
no 6 o'clock news,
no nothing!

out of concern, my Grandparents sent me 7 long blocks
through throngs of onlookers and searing heat,
to check on the welfare of my Aunt Rosa,
reclusive!
living alone, in a small Creole cottage (right up against the refinery
fence),

someone must have been looking down,
sparing both her and her home from the ravages of the flames,
spared by happenstance or piety?
for us, the question never arose,
the fire burned for 3 days straight,
kept everyone on edge,

"I guess it was just the cost of doing business,"

later that year, the Plastics factory fire, (right next door to
our house), was more like a marshmallow roast than a real fire, like the
refinery, while the fire still smoldered, we like good citizens helped
ourselves to: plastic cups, saucers, salad tongs and compartmentalized plates,
plates good for keeping the foods that you like away from
the ones that you don't

we had no complaints!

the Aluminum factory never caught on fire,

the trains that crossed over the trestle never derailed
spilling their mysterious cargo into the river,

never spoiled our swimming hole or favorite fishing spot,

thinking back,
we lost a lot of folks in our neighborhood,

"it never raised an eyebrow?"
"in those days people just died early"

"nothing really happens here!"

to us, it was,
Just Another Day in the Neighborhood.

No One Ever Tells You

Grown folks always have a way of looking out for kids
but consistently forget to tell kids to look out!

when you become big enough to go someplace by yourself,
grown folks are quick to give you directions to the places
that you want to go,
rarely do they give you instructions on the safest way
to get there,

for instance,
there is the traffic signal at the corner,
standing like a stern Grandmother,
"a woman of few words"
she gives no hugs!
choosing rather to protect you with her mechanical arms
and reassuring winks,

when exploring, kids tend to see blocks as miles and miles
as sightless safaris into the unknown,

a Saturday afternoon jaunt to the movies
(of course alone)
was fraught with danger,

no one ever mentions the resident neighborhood troll,
defiantly standing guard over all paths between you and
the movie theater,
the toll-taking troll was a thin shadow of a boy,
callous in his approach,
deadly in his intent to extract a
fare from you,
the price for passing through his territory,

as I moved toward my destination,
I couldn't help but notice the rage that was building up
inside of me,
to boot, something was making my eyes water!

"damn that little bully!"
"Oops! Better watch my mouth"
"Darn that little bully!"
"That cowardly little shit!"

have I forgotten to mention the big ferocious dog behind
the short picket fence?

a mere three blocks from the movies was a fragrant maze
of alleyways,
a shortcut paved with broken glass
inhabited by semiconscious winos and mange-ridden dogs,
all seeking shelter from public ridicule, scrutiny and scorn,

dodging the minefield of mumbling mouths and snapping canines,
I stepped from the alleyway onto the street,

gleefully, I rushed to the front door of the theater
only to be firmly intercepted by the theater manager,

confidently, I said "Sir what movie is playing today?"
his resounding response was"no kids under seventeen
admitted without being accompanied by a parent or Legal Guardian!"

performing a nearly perfect about face,
I headed for home all the time thinking,

"it sure would be nice to have some company to walk me back home"

now the streets are quiet,
the drunks are on their way to the local flophouse,
save one!
my Uncle Claude, God bless him!
he is on his way to our house for dinner,

the big vicious dog is securely stowed in his backyard
behind a locked gate,

the neighborhood troll having made enough money from
his exploits is on his way to the movie theater,
"boy will he be surprised!"

avoiding the shadows cast,
I cautiously move past,
lampposts and telephone poles along the way,

in the final stretch for home,
I pause to reflect,
that in time, all of this will change,

progress will replace familiar landmarks,
vague memories of youth will paint incomplete pictures of life's
experiences,

to think that this is yet another of those things that no
one ever tells you.

Down the Road

It was still, and hot,
as only a summer Perris afternoon can be,

the sandy arroyo soil was mounded with red ants,
standing tall to avoid contact with the scorching ground,

flies buzzed in confused circles,
as if blinded by the rising waves of heat,

in the deep barbecue pit dug by my Uncle,
smiling embers challenged all who dared approach,

down the road the general store laid,
a good mile in the distance,
there I stood barely nine years old,
three dollars in my pocket and a note in my hand,

"It's not far," said my Uncle with a reassuring laugh,
"Stay on the road so we can see you," reminded my Aunt,

a path through the sagebrush and fox-tails was my chosen
route, determined to avoid the man-made quicksand of the
interstate,

I stepped through the grass and scrub portal alive with the sage like
smell of cornbread dressing,
and back again as if by magic,

standing arm outstretched,
smiling, I handed my Uncle the brown paper bag with the
change rattling inside,
slowly, ever so slowly, my Uncle looked up the road,
then back at me,

puzzled, I froze,
dragging me across the road to the field,
with a fuming shout my Uncle said,
"Saved your feet and exposed your behind!"

"Look in the bushes, boy, look in the bushes,
just coiled up, waiting,
lucky for you it's too hot to bite,
how you gonna go next time?"

"Next time?"

"Yes, next time?"

"Down the road sir, down the road."

They Came in Droves

They came in droves to visit my Grandfather,
sun ripened in California, but all sprouted
some place else,

well dressed in gabardine, with subdued flowered shirts,
Panama hats in summer,
sharply creased felts at other times,

sometimes they came on Saturday afternoons,
often, early on Friday evenings,

always respectful, always laughing,
hand-rolled Cuban cigars ritually lit upon entering,
the front door,

they always retired to the kitchen where my Great-Grandmother lingered,
all conversation waited patiently for her departure,
as if by magic, shot glasses appeared in each well-manicured hand, some
filled with Four Roses,others filled with Old Crow,

my dog and I always watched silently from the service porch,
listening as the dominoes slapped (lively) on the table,
taunting one another as only friends can do,

the light in the kitchen grew brighter as the hour got later,
I never knew who won those games or how those stories ended,
I never even figured out who kept putting me to bed,
must have been Uncle Big Boy with his Havana stogie

and his stuttering laugh,
the next day I always asked my dog to tell me,
how the stories ended, who won those games,
and where the glasses of whiskey came from,

but all I ever figured out was,
they came in droves to visit my Grandfather.

Time Knows

My Great-Grandfather sat in the same sweltering heat,

before knowing me,

time knows,

here I sit in the same heat,

no longer knowing him,

time knows,

flies circling, gnats nipping,

out-back bayou fog hanging low off the water,

Spanish moss, draping from stately Oak Trees,

lining the walkway to the Big House,

time knows,

the river,

the same river, flows,

neither greeting nor bidding farewell,

brother gone,

sister never to be seen again,

casks of wine,

Parisian finery,

ain't the same as family,

just cargo on the river,

time knows,

the stars that all Grandfathers knew,

are the same stars,

shining long, ever so long,

before there were Grandfathers.

Time knows.

Not Knowing

Not knowing my father,

is contained,

in the phantom,

of cloistered whispers,

a permanent irritant,

the constant grinding,

heart against mind,

a barren oyster,

creating pain,

not producing a pearl.

Who was that Masked Man?

Anxious fingers, adjust full-face masks on shadowed
figures,

howling harlots, walking the street from dusk til dawn,
transform the intoxicated waltz of the night,

misguided steps of gentleman callers, sons of toe-tapping
transients, mimic the malaise of midnight minuets,

prognosticating pimps, hawkers of exotic wares,
leaning on lamp posts, practice predetermined poses,

the witching hour wanes, whisking away all vestiges of
dignity and privilege,

cobblestones clamor, worn thin by the muted sounds of
faltering footsteps,

haggard hordes, gorged on the feast and sights of Mardi
Gras, stagger home,

the room is empty,

menacing memories see only the face in the mirror,
not the man behind the mask.

Auntie Grace's Afghan

When I was sick,
I kept Auntie Grace close to me,
she had always been a member of our family,
soft, reliable, available,
a diversity of colors,
skillfully set upon a zig zag weave,
a faithful friend,
a cozy fireplace companion,
providing my wife warmth and comfort during the long cold grey days of winter,
our cat, also loved and embraced Auntie Grace,
finding delight, in attacking her fringed borders,
napping in her outstretched arms,
when our son was young and recovering from a football injury,
Auntie Grace never left his side,
you might say," she had us covered"
now, she is doing the same for me,
24 x 7 (if needed)
soft, reliable, available,
I'm getting better, soon to be well,
Auntie Grace,
will not be retired,
She will be gently,
washed, fluffed, folded,
respectfully, stored deep in the recesses of a cedar chest,
it seems a shame to leave her alone!
from time to time, I will peek in on her,
just to see how she is doing,
I will come away satisfied,
knowing that,
Auntie Grace,
will always be a member of our family,
soft, reliable, available.

Conversations at Cafe Du Monde

As we sat eating Beignets in the midst of quiet conversation,
the muffled voices of tourist's feet, fell upon cobblestone walkways,
bringing a new sense of rhythm to the sounds of the City,

languishing in our peripheral vision, scurrying waves of faceless
humanity cut through the afternoon shadows,
playing like memories on a bed sheet movie screen,

in a crowd, yet alone, our conversation, uninterrupted,
we searched the familiar faces of strangers,
looking, in this place, for a vestige of my youth,

you sipped a latte,
meaning no disrespect to a "Coffee" only tradition,
I alone, struggling shamefully to hide the "Green Tea" stain on my napkin,

while the wafting smells of the street unceremoniously stepped in
to join our conversation,
we talked,
gazing at life like starstruck teenagers,

outside, on a sun-broiled dark green metal bench,
conversations abound, judging the prowess of street musicians and
their choice of musical selections,

in the absurdity of the moment,
standing in a reserved space, next to the street side of Cafe Du
Monde,

an itinerant trombone player (New Orleans born and bred),

oblivious to time and place,

spontaneously broke into his musical and vocal rendition of "Do
You Know What It Means to Miss New Orleans,"
in the midst of conversation, nobody noticed,

the hour tolls,
the fading light seems to brings forth Spirits,
descending in memory like silhouettes from times past,

the Spirits of the Living and the Dead walk the promenade
hand in hand,

each guiding the other through moments past, and those yet to come,

words not spoken,
in time,
will become fresh brewed steaming cups of Cafe Au Lait,
powdered faces and hands will grasp fresh baked Beignets,

a still life,
the center piece for cherished memories,
of conversations at Cafe Du Monde.

Envy

From the day that I took my first step,
I knew that I must have those shoes,

those shoes?
no! not those shoes, my shoes!

the shoes that I wanted,
were handsomely displayed,
in the front window at Maison Blanche(an uptown department store),
at the end of Canal Street,

there they were, shiny and new, firmly affixed to the feet
of a shop worn mannequin,

now, these were no ordinary shoes,
not like those Kansas City Rockers and Stacy Adams cap-
toes that gamblers and fast people wore,

No Sir!
the shoes that I wanted were dignified and special,
the shoes of respectable people,

these weren't just anybody's shoes,
No indeed!
they were somebody's shoes

my Grandfather, had always owned a pair of those shoes,
Ox Blood in color, with perfect stitching, full leather soles
and Cat's Paw heels,
shoes fit for stepping out and being noticed,

my Uncles likewise, all owned a pair of those shoes,
some in Royal Tans and others in Ebonies,
but always those shoes,

how I envied those grownups and their magnificent shoes,
the same type of shoes that I would someday hope to own!

now looking at those shoes got me to thinking,

would I have to be as old or work as hard as my
Grandfather just to get those shoes?

would I have to go to War and lose my leg as my Uncle
did just to get those shoes?

If so, what would I do with the other shoe?

the last time I went to look at the shoes in the department
store display window, both the mannequin and the shoes
were gone,

oddly enough, I was glad!

just to think,

I saved money all of those years to buy my shoes,
but when it came time to buy them,
I was unwilling to pay the cost of owning those shoes.

Uncle Blue

(In that shadowed moment when wakefulness is fitful and sleep is a hill yet to climb,
I think of Uncle Blue.)
In my sleepless fog,
I become a kid, playing in the street,
again, listening for "a come on and hear moment,"
a pulsating pounding,
a boom, boom, boom, da,da,da,da,boom,
a captivating beat,
struck upon two 5-gallon discarded olive-oil cans,

from the corner of my eye,
I catch an unmistakable sight,
Uncle Blue in full stride,
cloaked in the oily sleeves of a threadbare coat,
dreadlocks snapping,
hobnail boots stepping,
flailing arms swinging,

a manila rope snaked through his belt loop,
holding together two disparate parts of a man,

thoughts swirling off tempo,
out of sync,
the beats of his drums,

right brain,
left brain,
a whole man,
marching,

one foot in the past,
the other frozen in the air,

in a time before the change,
older folks knew him by his given name,

we knew him only as Uncle Blue,

he passed away more than 60 years ago,
silence filled the void,
the rhythmic joy of his existence muffled,

gentrification, a modern day raising of the dead,
filled the spaces where he once roamed,

no more boom, boom, boom, da,da,da,da,boom,

the predictable staccatoed voices of crowded streets,
now speak for Uncle Blue,

"eccentrics no longer welcomed!"

boom, boom, boom, da,da,da,da,boom.

Edmonds in the Dead of Winter

Sea Gulls still harass diners at seaside cafes,

their calls are shrill, with chattering bills
as they break the winter grey,

neither winter snow, nor a northern blow,
churning whitecaps like heads on beer,

can sink our hope, or make us mope, because
wintertime is here,

no one in Edmonds cries, when Autumn dies,
and Winter comes to town,

we just throw another log on the fire,
and batten our hatches down,

I grab my old Eddie Bauer,
and get ready for the fight,
with Sorrels upon my feet,

I step outside with a sense of pride
and go boldly into the night.

The City at 4:04 am

Carnival masks remain on shelves,
more admired than worn,

wrought-iron skirts twist around balconies,
mimic the course of the river,

the bank of hard-times remains open,
solvent,
customer rich,
cash poor,

Amoco!
has come and gone,
"Filler up!"

I mean:
hotel rooms,
restaurants,
taxis,
merchants pockets,
nightclubs,
cans for the homeless,

employment and unemployment lines are of equal length,
each moving with appreciation and disappointment,

my buddy somewhere past fifty,
smiles at a young lady strolling through the French Quarters,

"Man I know what's beautiful," he says,
"Yea," I say, "but I know what's available,"

the ever pressing rain waits for breaks in the overhead string of awnings and
balconies,
waiting for opportunities to attack wandering tourist separated from rental cars,

taxi drivers smirk,
remaining out of sight,
allowing merchants to sell umbrellas and disposable raincoats,

times are hard!
money scarce,
pride and respect are on the line,
promoters are trying to turn Cajun culture into a theme park,

the sacred rites of Voudin,
gift of Mother Africa,
into a sideshow attraction,

in the end,
visitors to New Orleans,
confused,
avoid "Bad neighborhoods" with good food,
choose to visit "Good neighborhoods with bad food."

Winter Sledding on my Hill

Fractured billows of smoke,
glide past ice-slick roads,

undeveloped fear,
prepares star cradles,
to assault the frozen winter phantom,

ignoring chores and favorite fare,
squires pay homage to the rights of passage,

scars are heroic,
falling is not failing,

matchlights pull shadows,
from the blinding darkness,

piercing screams,
shatter the frigid night air,
parents hearts, as well,

laughter brings relief,

wet clothes, in the laundry room,
brings peace, even in times of war.

Must

I must remember the things that I forgot,
for if I fail to do so,
remembering would have been for naught.
you didn't live on my street,
surrounded by : factories, an oil refinery, an upholstery supply company, a commercial
laundry, the L.A. Pie Company, trains, river sounds,
urban, yet disconnected, from sights, sounds, activities and the sophistication of the
city's heart,
early morning spring aromas wafting across the tracks bring back a memory,
a memory, an annual reprieve, overpowering the sweet fragrance of magnolias and
bouganvillas,
an escape from the tedious confined movements of familiar faces,
a momentary pause in the maddening repetition, screen doors slamming,
living on the wrong side of the tracks can have its advantages,
once a year, elephants walked down my street,
parading in tow, trunk grasping tail, a side to side rhythmic waddle,
porch swings fill, tightly packed,
families huddled together against the fearful entanglement of the passing spectacle,
anticipating, the bone rattling roar of the lions,
the clank of time-worn wooden wheels on cages,
sway back and forth upon the cobblestones and potholes of benign neglect,
rusting bars, spread apart,
lions reach out,
paw the air,
create a fearful silence,
a silence soon broken by uncontrollable laughter,
children pointing, gleefully admiring the humorous humps on the backs of camels,
older folks in the neighborhood take a moment to reflect,
the poor roustabout, obediently following behind the elephants,
broad shovel in hand,
the circus passing by, like life, leaves ruts, worn in the road,
the continuous flow from flatbed cars in the rail-yard to the tent site, move along the
confined corridors of separation,
strong arms working in unison, provide work for locals, strain against giant manila
ropes, erect magic edifices on vacant lots,

as days pass the return of the elephants draw little attention,
a weary lackluster movement of men and beast become a distant memory,

I must remember the joy, the pride, of the annual parade, the exclusive property of
neighborhoods on the wrong side of the tracks.

Valentine (The Search)

It's Valentine's Day,

my Grandson sits,

pained by a broken heart,

love lost, or temporarily interrupted?

my efforts to console,

fall short,

thoughts drift off subject,

I search deep within,

grasping for the strength of hands,

hands,that brought me comfort,

in my thoughts,

I perceive an insurmountable chasm,

separating the shaded memories of yesterday,

from the glaring truths of today,

what happened to the quintessential Grandmother and Grandfather?

have Grandmothers become unrecognizable,

disguising the looks and appearance of old age,

badges of maturity and wisdom,

sloughed off,

no more dowdy attire,

white hair, wizen look,

gone!

no more Grandma Fritz, Grandma Lula,

not even Gumma,

have grandmothers fallen out of favor?

artificial knees and hips,

displace the artful and affable Grandma waddle,

the charm, grace, gone!

the strength, warmth of spirit from my youth,

faded into obscurity,

has the rock become a stone?

today, Grandfathers drive snappy new cars,

don baseball caps, use products to keep the grey away,

hide or disguise balding heads,

no bib overalls,

no Stetson hats,

no more tipping your hat to a lady,

no longer teaching grandchildren,

what they need to know,

teaching only,

what they want them to know,

strong gnarly hands,

with a finger or two missing,

a thing of the past,

no more reading Aesop's fables,

no more telling outrageous lies,

while attempt to holding back a twinkle in their eyes,

at 73 here I sit,

a grandfather,

decked out in my LL Bean jeans, Henley, Fitbit, and Keen Sandals,

passing time,

time,until I can put on my baseball cap,

slip into my Joseph Abboud jacket,

drive my SUV to the store,

I will spend time,

time,peering down,

every aisle,

searching for the quintessential grandmother or grandfather,

will memories of the past,

rising and falling with the tide,

console my grandson?

Valentine's day is a day of the heart,

the saint for whom the holiday is named,

is obscure,

as are the ways,

to treat the trials and tribulations of the heart.

A Gathering around the Family Piano

There was a wholeness in the family's dysfunction,

an orchestrated coming together of disparate parts,

everyone had a moment,

an opportunity,

a responsibility,

a role to play,

a need to pull genius from the air,

some sang,

some played,

All cared about the music,

"Jazz was in their souls!"

the sounds,

languid and earthy,

a blues shout,

a gospel note,

a classical riff,

an alcoholic musing,

syncopated inebriation,

delivering pace to the flowing melody line,

moving in and out,

music swirling like a catfight in a smoke-filled box,

an ever-present stupor,

the curse of addiction woven deep into the fabric of family and New Orleans culture, glasses too full,

"...far too often,"

they all drank to that!

as a child I sat curious,

listening,

gathered close to smell the harmony of voices,

feel the punctuated pounding of cigarette-stained piano keys,

keys scorched by blazing fingers,

leaping across the notes,

music competing with kitchen aromas:

Gumbo boiling,

rice steaming,

eyes weeping,

too much pepper,

too much cigarette smoke,

a bubbling cauldron,

angels and devils mixing,

a potent brew of humanity,

a family whole in their dysfunction,

looking back,

the steps of time separate the memory from the event,

leaving only a dim light burning.

Snohomish Valley Autumn
(Why I love this town)

Hot air balloons are up,

the river is down,

the autumn sunset obscures the signs,
pointing the way to Stocker's farm,
around the curve,
Marsh Road lays,
amidst plowed fields,
one side awash in people, scavenging,
for dew-laden pumpkins,
the other,
a verdant carpet,
covering the fallow earth,
from trees,
screaming leaves parachute,
performing pirouettes,
to avoid hard landings,
touching down,
amidst the rancorous laughter,
of a snickering breeze,

in autumn,

people seem to move at a brisker pace,
the crowds of tourists, (on First Street),
have become sparse,
allowing locals to reclaim their territory
the town heralds the return of its locals

extolling the virtues of leisurely walks along the river,
familiar haunts are now filled with neighborly gossip,
conversations regarding the town's quaintness have
ceased,
isn't it uncanny, how the cobblestones,
of our town have their own way,
of precisely fitting your stride,
whether you are drunk or sober,

that people tend to recognize you,
because of where you are,
not who you are,
that no one need ask for directions, even if lost,

if you were to ask me,
what is my favorite thing about autumn?
it would be,
it never fails to remind me,
why I love this town.

Remembering My Grandfather

As time passes,
the silent snowfall,
nestles deep,
branching from trees to roof top eves,
gathering in spaces,
time tied to memories,
memories to time,
the bristles of my artist brush, stiff, wiry, like my Grandpa's
beard, paint memories of times past,
Grandpa, I can no longer touch you,
I can only touch the things that you touched,
hold the things that you held,
I still have your pocket watch,
a gold 21-jewel Bulova,
silent like your voice,
stored, deep, in the recesses of a top dresser drawer,
daily, I give 22 precise turns on the crown,
setting in motion,
an awakening, anticipated,
a slumber broken,
the breath of each movement,
a gift celebrated,
the coming of memories,
synced with time,
soon,
ticking without notice,
the heartbeat of time,
the memory of your voice,
fading, deep into the silent snowfall.

Sun Sets in the Southwest

Reasonable Expectations?
(Sarcasm)

Damn it, speak English!

when you cross that border to come here,
speak English!

when we cross that border to go there,
speak English!

when we barter for those colorful little trinkets,
speak English!

when skilled Mexican hands perform delicate dental
procedures in our American mouths,
speak English!

when we are lying helpless in the midst of one of those
little dark and dingy recovery rooms,
musing over our newly sculpted face-lift and bargain tummy tuck,
speak English!

if by chance, one of us wants to learn Spanish from one of you,
speak English!

Damn it, speak English!

Carajo! Ya habla en inglés!

Reasonable Expectations Revisited

Show some respect Arizona!

Respect,
the fact that the Southwest owes the vitality of its cultural
roots to the Mexican people,

Respect,
the language and people from whom you so shamelessly use as a
source for naming your streets and housing developments,

Show some respect Mexico!

Respect,
the indigenous people,
stop looking down on them,
They are your heart,

Respect,
the dark-skinned people of the Costa Chica,
stop demoralizing and belittling them,
They are your soul,

Respect,
Your people, Mexico!
give them a reason to want to stay home.

I Love the Desert but I can't Stand the Heat

I can't stand the heat of intolerance,
that fans the flames of hate,

I can't stand the heat of ignorance,
that melts the heart of trust,

I can't stand the oppressive heat,
that shrink wraps the brain,
causing narrow mindedness,

the Imax vision of stars,
punctuate the indigo face of night,

panoramic parades of cacti,
gallivant across the desert landscape,

in the distance a lone Coyote howls.

Men who put the "Boy" in Cowboy

Arizona is a place where all white men over 60, sound like Gabby Hayes,

the philosophy of the day, "if you ain't for us then you're agin us,"

favorite pastime, mispronouncing as many Spanish words as English words,

the law is for them, not us!

Global Warming is a lie and so was Brokeback Mountain,

Rush Limbaugh and Sheriff Joe Arpaio are modern day prophets,

if it ain't red meat
it ain't fit to eat

what ever happened to Woodrow Wilson?

all politics are local

the second most important moment in your life, is getting your first gun,
the most important moment in your life, is getting your first box of ammunition,

we don't trust the Government,
but we are damn proud to be American!

it's ok to be a poet,
thanks Baxter Black!
we appreciate the painted skies of our over the mountains sunsets,
the whisper of the wind,
a colt whinnying,
critters large and small,
a lizard climbing an adobe wall,
we are harsh and tough,
our skin leathered,
our manners rough,
but our hearts are full of love,
nightly on our knees we kneel
to thank the man above,
don't them darn Coyotes ever sleep?
some shuteye
some shuteye
before the lifestyle of a Cowboy
withers,
dies.

El Dormido Con Tres Perros
(The Sleeping Man with 3 Dogs)

The ride to Nogales,
 was on a smooth road,

the summer sky,
cloudless,

the land alluring,

to the east, in the distance,
we could see an off white colored dome,
perched precariously on top of Mount Wrightson,

anxiously,
we watched the miles turn into kilometers,

I was traveling, South to Mexico,
to seek an Optometrist,
to reverse the unintended consequence of dropping my glass
spectacles on an unforgiving tile floor,

my wife, on the other hand, was traveling to Mexico to make
peace with the land,

25 years ago,
a land, without permission,
temporarily sped up her digestive system,
abscessed her tooth,
ubiquitously placed all manner of crawling creatures
in her hotel room to torment her,
all to the delight of the fine citizens of the Republic of Mexico,

our Son had neither misfortune to correct nor relationships to mend,

being fluent of tongue,
he possesses a brazen and unabashed distaste for borders,
particularly those that separate people and ideas from each other,

crossing the border on foot,
we made serpentine movements through the crowded marketplace,
touching both the commerce and mundane activities of the
people of Nogales,

in the midst of a quiet moment,
the ordered chaos of the streets slowly carouseled around a
sleeping man
with 3 dogs,

he wore a smile cleaner than; his clothes, his hair, his face
and cleaner than his dogs,
He neither begged, sold goods,
nor performed for the masses,

in the streets he was exposed,
but safe,

anonymous,
but well known,

he was performance art,
at its best,

in an entrance way to an alley,
he lay upon the cobblestone street,

ignored,
like a pebble in the shoe of a legless man.

Because you are Family

Wind I talk to you because you are family,
I hear your mournful moan,
feel the destructive force of your rage,
yet I talk to you because you are family,

Rain I talk to you because you are family,
I feel the refreshing drops of perspiration from your
furrowed brow,
when you are gone too long the land of my spirit becomes
parched,
and I lament,
when you come too often, I drown in your sorrow,
still I talk to you because you are family,

Sky I talk to you because you are family,
you draw me beyond the edges of my thoughts,
you cleverly conceal the monsters present in the daytime
under your cloak of darkness,
I fear you,
however, we remain on speaking terms because we are family.

Too Hot to Handle

Liberated Women

Liberated women digging in the dirt,
free to try,
free to succeed or fail,

Liberated women digging in the dirt,

tugging on a tree,
unyielding in its stand,
firmly planted in the ground,
is this what the struggle was all about?
the sacrifice ?
the hardships?
the pain?

Liberated women digging in the dirt.

The Plight of Old Black Women

Alone and beyond their usefulness; some turn inward,

their inner loneliness, bound up and coddled by childhood
memories, often gives rise to flights of fancy,

most struggle to recall endearing moments,
harkening back to a time in an obscured but glorious past,
a time, when they were respectively referred to as Ma'am,
Mother, Auntie, Big Mama, or on the rarest occasions, Mrs.,

now an occasional "hey you," " that old woman," or " that
old colored woman," is all the attention that some of them get,

their families! where are their families?
Out, Living life!
this will continue to be the plan until they, themselves, are struck
by the blessings of old age,
then what?

Old Black Women, once stood as fortresses of dignity, pride and stability,
they were the backbone of families, the pride of communities, the foundations of the
church,

now as faceless discarded relics of a bygone era,
they are set aside to collect dust,
in the cutting shadows, where walls converge.

Why Don't You Get it?

Looking, I no longer see me in you,
I only see you,

it's an old trick,
don't you get it?

it was always our neighborhood,
our Barrio,
our Hood,

now it's your street,
your territory,
your area code?

it's still an old trick,
don't you get it?

Norteños
Sureños
Bloods
Crips

your gang violence, your self-destruction,
is limiting your future, scarring your past and
destroying the moment,

My Brothers, you are being used!

divide and conquer not divide and share:
in prisons
in neighborhoods
in minds and in hearts

it worked all too well in those old slavery days,

why not now!
It's an old trick, why don't you get it?

Actions that Bring Men to Tears

I cried for their freedom,
two hundred and fifty thousand strong,

not a stone lifted,
a bullet fired,
freedom won from the unity of song,

I cried for their freedom,
as men in tanks, amassed at the edge of town,

I prayed for their safety,
as they held hands,
surrounding the broadcast tower,
standing their ground,

I wept for joy,
when their flag, was again raised in 1991,
their oppressors shamed into submission,
tyranny on the run,

I smiled when I heard their story,
while standing in their midst,

Estonia, a nation of unity,
has defeated the iron fist.

Stockholm Summer

Stockholm Summer,

3 days of sunshine,

1 day of rain,

the remainder,

a light drizzle,

faces obscured,

upon this land,

the fate of fortune falls,

the new identity of Sweden,

lies behind faces,

no longer strangers to the land,

a grand bargain,

to socialize caring,

by the sweat of each brow,

how did common sense,

seize these stewards of the north,

who in the bleakest of times see only shadows,

while we see only the bleakest of times,

proud warriors,

placing the legacy of war into the past,

the winter provides a time to reflect,

the midnight sun,

or midnight son of a bitch,

if it won't let you sleep,

keeps a watchful eye on progress,

while ponderous thoughts,

of companions lost,

stir memories from the deep.

St. Louis Twister (1988)

Elemental predators,
twist and howl,
scouring the prairies,
of America's forgotten lands,

campaigning in the streets,
sights set against God-fearing unionist, with domestic cars,
converting housing from affordable to disposable,

"Old News Boy Day" will not be spoiled,
by novel thoughts of underground housing,
or bridge maintenance,

the still believers,
broken and weary,
find solace in a bad call at Busch Stadium,

the Gateway Arch, gives Alton a window,
on our prosperity,

the Admiral, cruising the river of red ink,
docks in a foreign port,

the river queen puts on a new face to attract suitors,
exhorting city fathers to lay bricks,
for the wind to walk on,

winter's salted roads,
spill over into old wounds,

in rural areas,
some remember the dark times,
and must hurry home,

politicians filibuster,
arms outstretched,
point to the heartland,
yet, failing to touch its soul.

Metamorphosis

The arms of winter hold tight,
embrace the land, restricting movement,
an eerie silence spreading far and near,
dreams of radiant shafts of light,
break the shadowed darkness of a winter's night,
a change is coming!
stasis awakens unto life,
through frigid air, raindrops fall,
transformed, crafted, individual works of art,
a change is coming,
spring, a time to get about one's business,
what is pupating inside the dark chambers of secrecy,
if a patriot walks into a room and a traitor walks out,
is that metamorphosis,or just false news?
a tale reminiscent of the Wizard of Oz ,
pay no attention to the man behind the President,
like the seasons,
we are all obligated, to change, from birth to death,
a transformation,
like:
water
to
ice:
to
steam,
a skeleton fully clothed, is not " the person",
spring is not winter,
summer is not fall,
it is the change,

the underpinning that is metamorphosis,
peace after war,
love after hate,
wisdom after folly,

meta, beyond,
morphosis, change,
the egg never looks like the chicken,
the wind never feels like the rain,
yet all fit, dangling,
like charms on a bracelet.

Why
(Racism)

The Cost of Doing Business

I want to be left alone,
with my memories,
undisturbed,
obligated,
to live with the painful parts of the past,
the truth of who I am,
who we are,
is hidden,
tucked away,
in obscure chambers of deceit,
our minds hear voices,
echoing,
from generations past,
they are the purveyors,
of false hope,
speaking like tiny stones,
rattling inside a tin can,
We were created here!
in this land,
not in Europe,
not on the continent of Africa,
but right here,
in this land!
We are the children of neglect:
the blue eyed,
green eyed,
cream colored,
high yellow,
marigny,
curly haired,
wavy haired,
progeny of the white man's bout,
with amnesia and himself,
homeless hybrids,
branded with your family name,
tied to you,
by blood and circumstance,
vilified bastards,
of shame and conquest,

You feel no allegiance toward us!
to you, we are merely,
the unintended consequences of your exploits,
you killed, spilled,
mixed blood, to make us,
yet you refuse,
to acknowledge, or accept us,
the legacy of slavery,
must not be judged merely by the depth of its pain,
but by the breadth of its neglect!

I am the blood of the slave and slave master!

A potent brew!

Father, tell us!

Where is our Moses?

And, where in the hell is our promised land?

It No Longer Matters

Your 1950's and my 1950's were not the same,

you were buying spiffy new cars,
living in cookie cutter tract homes,
watching weekly episodes of Ozzie and Harriet,

you were the new face of success,

we were still the faces on boxes of pancake mix, Cream-O-Wheat,
bags of rice and Abba-Zabbas,

we ran on the railroad on the likes of the Sunset Limited
and the Super Chief,
changed your sheets in Pullman berths, serving your every need,

you were free to move about the country,

we continued to be terrified by public signs in The South,
saying "if you can't read, run,"

experiences of my 1960's and yours were definitely not the same,

you were asleep,
we were just waking up,

The Brothers and Sisters that I knew in the 1960's were
dedicated to getting respect,

they were not running around with guns in their hands,
as many thought,
but with ideas in their heads,

we lived in perilous times,
forcing us to shout in private places to be heard,
and to whisper in public places not to be detected,

your life and mine were akin to watching a double feature at a drive-in,
each screen showing a different movie,

ours in color,
yours in black and white,

it no longer matters!
it's the 21st century,

now, here we are up the same creek,
neither of us having enough money to buy a paddle.

We Must Really Be Important

I have always been convinced that the word "Love"
was the most pervasive and admired theme in the lyrical content
of American Music,
Not so!
after careful study, I have come to realize that the use of the word "Darkie"
in popular songs of the 19th and 20th centuries, can and does give "Love"
a run for its money,
You had us "Beating our Feet Down on the Mississippi Mud"
we weren't allowed to track it into your homes,
(we lived in houses, You lived in homes)
You had us hanging out "Way Down Upon the Suwanee River" fortunately, we
never got wet or lost,
(from being far, far away and scared)
You grew to become nostalgic for" Old Black Joe"
true he never was a" Darkie"
(just old and Black)
while "Sailing Along on Moonlight Bay"
You were being entertained by singing "Darkies" who were in the middle of the
ocean,
(remember we can't swim)

It's been said that the greatest gift is "Love"
according to some,
the greatest gift is "Darkies"

We Must Really Be Important.

The County Line

I watched a young black girl walk,
along the side of a suburban road,
two years ago rural,

musing on the change of color in our town,
I recall that, color had come only in the fall,

I drove, watching those well-dressed, dignified steps,
fade into the distance,

ringed mist glowed around the morning sun,
crackling the memory of a cross burning in our town.

Travel

My decision to travel, is more than the when, where or how,
I am not dependent on a travel agency,
my spirit guide is history,
unflinching, ingrained, deep, dark, dank, unforgiving,

I grew up listening to The Grand Ole Opry,
each Saturday night, ears glued to an old Philco radio,
my grandparents and I listened, laughed, sang,

in our minds,
We could see Cousin Minnie Pearl decked out in her freshly starched gingham
dress, sporting a straw sun hat, price tag still attached,

We could hear the sweet drawl of Judy Canova,
envision pig tails hanging, touching the front of her pinafore,
beneath, feet sheltered by over sized scuffed brogans,

unforgettable, the preachy oratories of Grandpa Jones,
filtered through corncob pipe smoke,
washing over a brand spanking new pair of overalls,

We knew them, they were us!

Grandma, we have cousins in Tennessee?
Uncle Jake has a brand new Packard?
We could travel to the Opry!

then the silence,
an ominous silence,
a calm before the storm,
a storm that never came,
hidden between frowns,
fidgeting, hand wringing,
lay a deep dark truth, old as time,

in the journey from childhood to old age, little has changed,
the road to various destinations, is still fraught with danger,
in some places, your money can buy you tolerance,
in others, no amount of money can offset the currency of hate,

daily I gaze upon the wall,
in my home office,
a place of refuge,
stringed instruments displayed on the wall,
hanging left to right:
Dobro, mandolin, 5 string banjo, classical guitar, dreadnought guitar,
all memories of The Opry,
a trip never taken,
lines never crossed,

for me travel planned is deeper than reaching into my wallet,
deeper than desires or dreams,
it is a reach into a deep, dark history,
silent,
a calm before the storm,
maps show 50 states,
for me there are far fewer,
deep, dark, silent.

That's What They Expect

"The Spook That Sat by the Door"
is still sitting,
but he is not in my way,

as a Black Man,
my life in corporate America was like being forced to
wear a newly starched white shirt but not being
allowed to get it wrinkled,

I could breathe the air in my own space,
but heaven forbid,
not in any other,

my opinion was never my own,
they never, I mean never, asked me what I thought,
only what I thought about "this" or "that"
but never what I really thought,

I was expected to ignore all insults,

I always had to be diplomatic,

why?
because I was a leader!

then why in the hell didn't they show some
leadership and stop insulting me!

over the years, I waited patiently for the day,
when they would give me so much money that I'd feel
guilty and want to give it back,
(they wouldn't be expecting that)

"The Invisible Man" has yet to be seen,

Then that's what they expect.

Eyes on Nature

Song of Green Woods

The cleric's voice rings foul,
against the silent sentinel,
winter stirs restless in the fallen leaves,
the high mountain pass shades,
the distant face of the sun,
wheat fields gloat in the fullness,
of moonlight,
fairies, sown on lost memories,
dance around the ringed fire,
pumpkins, full-term,
lay dew-laden, in hand turned soil,
crystal tears relieve the pain,
of midnight skies,
the bridge lies low,
gently stroking the wayward waters,
of lost generations,
highways push valleys aside,
tearing spirits from trees,
Eagles roost on the tails of comets,
leaving hunters abandoned.

Drifting

When I see water,
a stream,
a river raging,
a silent brook,
a stormy sea,

I see the clarity of mind-flowing,
unbridled,
unburdened,

flowing like the sands of time through splayed fingers,

thoughts not constricted or firmly held in vessels of consciousness,

free-flowing from place to place,
riding the waves of experience,

changing, ever changing,
with the rise and fall of aging tides,

drifting,
ever-drifting.

Spring Under the Cover of Night

Under the cover of night, who was out prowling around,
shaking branches, disturbing the trees, rustling the bushes, spreading the ground-
cover,

you go to bed and get up and there it is!
trees with leaves, flowers with vibrant colors, and those pain in the butt dandelions,

now the birds wake up early, cheerful chirps offset the noise of early morning traffic,

looking out the window, I spy a spindly lone green stem growing in the window
box, my wife says it's a weed,

I prefer,
to call it,
spring under the cover of night.

Fall Colors

Autumn is a time of freedom,

a time to step outside of the box!

a time for trees to stand up and be noticed,

a time to disregard subtleties,

a time to change nature's social order!

a time for trees to escape from the monochromatic
nightmare and boredom of ubiquitous surly green leaves,

a time for a wardrobe change!

a time for tree leaves to sport fashionable color: sunlit
crimsons, tangerine tinged golds, and caramel apple browns,

a time of glorious pageantry,

a time for autumn's chill to smugly turn a cold shoulder to
the languishing presence of summer,

in the waning moments of the season, trees remember that
autumn is their only ally,
a staunch supporter of fall colors' right to exist,

as the onslaught of winter cavalierly enslaves the
landscape and stealthily silences woodland voices,

a solitary leaf still flush with color lies stoically upon
freshly fallen snow.

Observations

Walk hand and hand with Nature
not a step beyond
nor a step behind.

> The gurgling voice of my pond is silent
> the pump is broken
> nothing calls the Birds to drink
> nor the Rabbits to rest.

The Desert wind blows
teaching the Trees to dance
and my bamboo wind chimes to sing.

> A Lizard hides behind the cushion of my chair
> behind the cushion of my chair a Lizard hides.

My neighbor cut down their Palo Verde tree
to improve the view
now when I wish to see the Tree whatever shall I do?

> Today a Road Runner stood curiously upon my block wall
> he saw me sitting
> he came ever so close
> leaving hastily, without uttering a single word
> perhaps tomorrow we shall talk.

A Raven breaks the silence with his loud call
the silence is broken by a Raven's loud call.

Winter Knocks

Upon my door a frosty knock,

how sweet the winter breath,

refreshing nostrils,

a damp comfort of season's change.

The Edmonds' Overnight Rain

Blurring the vision of man-made portals,
rhythmic pulses created by the overnight rain,
fall on rooftop skylights,
owning the night,
a distant train rumbles,
swaying back and forth,
cutting a swath through shoreline mist and fog,
in the vapored darkness, muted voices cry out,
Freight!
Amtrak!
Sounder!
the hour is late,
no one complains,
sleepers sleep,
the tide is unaffected,
the overnight rain,
washes the face of the moon,
refreshing its glow,
relieving the burden of street sweepers,
the fountain in the central roundabout sparkles as if new.

Reflections

Midwinter sunlight filters through barren trees,
watching as cars pass below,
a family of crows stand on bare branches,
peering down, undisturbed,

remnants of recent rains,
cast familiar images as crows gaze into puddles,

Crows are a curious lot:
wise, pensive, reflective, staying above the fray,

life in urban treetops creates a complex association,
an entanglement of branches and wires...

not unlike the daily activities of men,
routines, obligations, and relationships occupy the everyday lives of crows,
time is merely the synchronized passing of sunrises and sunsets,
blowing winds bring the seasons,

No one is homeless!

perhaps on a clear autumn night, when gazing at the stars,
we will see both the faces of men and crows painted on the surface of a bright harvest
moon.

but for now, we will collect our thoughts,
reflecting on who we are,

while crows rest on barren branches as cars pass below.

Making Your Presence Known

I miss your voices,
flying overhead,
familiar honks,
distant and near,

sounds filtering through the subtle shadows of autumn,

your voices comforting and reassuring,
masking the silent screams of falling leaves,

you bring to mind, frolicking memories of summer, now gone,
your departure, a harbinger of the soft winter silence, yet to come,

gazing upward, you appear as a well disciplined mass,
marching across the sky,
off to conquer new lands,

eerie shadows falling upon the landscape, below,
make your presence known.

Fall Collection

My eyes speak to the flashing colors,
of the changing seasons,

trafficked in the autumn corridor,
shadowed in a tranquil light,

filtered through cracks,
of winter's reserve,

final splurges,
set for winter storehouse raids,
line pantry shelves,

sun-pressed clouds,
obscure views of furrowed fields,

hammers fall,
scented by fires of toiled reward,

winds scream,
soon to whisper,

the slumber queen,
dances in tight circles,
capturing the children of autumn leisure.

The Mist

The Pacific Northwest mist,

some rejoice,

some complain,

the mist persists.

Spring (Predictability of Butterflies and Bumble Bees)

Spring,

a crack in the winter gloom,

raising of the shade,

the breath of a breeze,

a gentle swirling,

playing hide and seek among the branches,

awakens the voice of wind chimes,

the eyes of curious men,

asleep, from shadows cast by the intoxication of moonlight,

reach inside,

to feel,

the winter loneliness,

reflected in the face of the pond,

ducks arrive,

revel in the embrace of water,

a gentle rocking back and forth,

brings comfort,

around the edges,

thoughts flit through the mind,

like the grace of a butterfly searching for the proper bloom,

Spring,

predictable,

steadfast,

like the hovering, of a bumble bee.

Day Dream

Peering over tree tops,
the moon captures,
the smile in God's eyes,

bidding farewell to the final sighs of winter,
the traveled mist of snow-blown fog, settles
on the valley floor,

the night eagle lands,
wiping clean,
the frozen face of mountains,
stranded above the clouds,

the window at the end of the hill,
opens,
letting the twilight breeze,
gently lift the shade of evening,

fires of dusk,
breathe a mystical glow,

the star magician winks,

Damn it!

I missed my exit.

Oars and Sails

A Gentle Wind

All I need is a gentle wind,
a wind at my back to blow slow and steady,

a wind upon which to set my sails,

not a passive wind,
nor a contentious wind,
but a gentle wind,

a wind to breathe life back into my sails,

I need a persuasive wind,

a wind capable of overcoming the slumbering spirits of the doldrums,

I need a powerful wind,
a wind to stay the fog-shrouded hand that seeks to blend
the horizon with the waterline,

I need a gentle wind,
a wind at my back to blow slow and steady,

I need a gentle wind,
a wind to help me navigate the seas of life.

The Lighthouse

To home they say as they signal land,

to sea weary captains and crew,

approaching port,

they judge not,

the mission sought,

the sea must have its due.

The Keys

The place that matches the dreams,
of a fertile mind,
communes nightly with custom,

drawing the shade,
the dowager of evening,
quiets the pastel faces of day,

adventure, embroiled in this humid place,
writhes lurid on cobblestone steps,

obsession with the past,
nostalgia plundered,
from rusting wrought iron balconies,
lures pirates from retirement,

bridges break at water's edge,
dower moon offsets,
the lauded encore of sunset,

wanderers showing preference for the open road,
pull the keys together,
like a string of pearls.

Amsterdam Dream

A steady rain,
a thunderous rumble,
then a roar,

a paparazzi flash of lighting,
across the canal,
shows the sign above the door,

your life is like a bad cup of coffee,
you can't stand the grind,

lightning flashes again,
a thousand commercials race across,
the landscape of your mind,
filling empty spaces, unlike an oasis,
in the land of endless grains of sand,
"this ain't your grandma's coffee"
it's from some far off,
exotic land,

a coffee shop,
a hotel room,
and
a prostitute,
walk into a bar,

"Not True"
but you stayed at a Holiday Inn once,

as your thoughts start to rise, like the steam from an expensive espresso machine,
you realize, "life is only good to the very last drop"

that zone,
that ponderous dream,
between, 1 cube or 2,
black or with cream,
surrounded by strangers
yet alone,
rub a dub dub,
there are no men in this tub,
you are still captive, in an Amsterdam coffee shop,
not in an Irish pub,

a remote nagging memory, in the back of your mind,
keeps reminding you,
of a different place,
a broader space,
an earlier time,

the shadow on the wall, is telling you,
it's getting late,
you are in good hands,
but not with Allstate,

"you deserve a break today"
as your cruise ship left without you,
and sails away,

did curiosity, bring you here?
did you have an item on your bucket list, yet to clear?

when you failed to see the Starbucks logo on the sign,
above the door,
why did you hesitate?
what made you stop?
it's a universal truth,
that they don't sell coffee,
in an Amsterdam coffee shop!

The Voice of the Seagull

Riding gracefully on wind currents,
dropping from the sky,
like leaves,
buffeted by an Autumn breeze,

the voices of seagulls calling,
challenging all frigates and schooners,
who dare,
to set ship's sails, upon the seas,

these sentinels of the sky,
take shameless delight,
out maneuvering the shadows, of billowing sails below,
the movement of clouds in flight,

soaring flocks jostle for position,
on the fragile edge of the slip,
silhouetted portraits above the isthmus,
rounding the Horn, pass the southern tip,

through the passage of time,
their voices heard,
from the tops of main masts' sails,
to the decks of wooden ships,
stronger than the coxswain's shout,
to the fall of perspiration's drips,

these beacons of the sky,
guide all worthy seamen,
to the ports at journey's end,

calling from sea to shore,
voices rings forever constant,
as the clamor of the blowing wind.

There She Blows

"There she blows"
the voice of a fog horn,
calling, from a distant place,

on all the seas her voice is known,
no one knows her face,

there are times, when the watchful eye of a lighthouse stare,
is the lesser choice,
a call to arms, the true protector,
lies in a familiar voice,

to fearful hearts, she speaks cautious words,
through the power of her blow,
to sailors who attend the sails
to the strokes of the oarsman's row,

an ancient threat,
the reaper's bet,
to hear the horn no more,

but steady as she goes,
through thickening fog,
and pints of grog,
this maven of the shore,

when I think of whales and seamen's tales,
and old sea dogs who spin yarns,

I'll think of waves and lives saved,
by the blowing of the horn.

Tall Ships Lost (Camden Harbor)

As I speak through trembling lips,
I wonder what kind of men,
go to sea on sailing ships,

I kneel not, yet I pray,
to protect these fools,
as they sail away,

to tropic lands
and
polar cold

they see themselves,
as seafarers bold,

a silent phantom,
sneaks, in the night,

sails by stars
and
light of moon bright

I wonder what kind of men go on sailing ships,

no longer do they sail for cargo port,

they sail for pleasure,

they sail for sport,

Oh! how I long for Tall Ships and
tales of seamen lost,

of Boatswain's sighting sextons,
on the North Star,

charting courses, by way,
of the Southern Cross,

bring back the Tall Ships,
this I pray,

no longer shall I call them fools
as they sail away.

Crossing the bay

Crossing the bay
I love the grey,

the grey,
that speaks of calm,
hidden fingered spires,
shadowed in the mist,
a curtained sheer,
across the face of day,

I love the grey,
upon the clock tower face,
a mystic touch,
a mariner's rhyme,
the winds of time,
stir memories,
hiding in this place,

I love the grey,
its foreboding presence,
lost souls shun,
the light of day,
fortunes and dreams lost,
in deference to the grey,

I love the grey,
the solitude of fog,
a silent weighty embrace,
cascading over the shoulders,
like a rain-soaked cloak, wet
plumes rising,
drift upward in the fog.
as puffs of chimney smoke,

dissipating thoughts linger,
as judgments fade,
into shades of grey,

shouts become,
whispers,

crossing The Bay,
I love the grey.

The Philosopher's Moment

I Believe

I believe Buddhists are close,
but they are not right,
they only understand,
the interconnectedness of all things,

I believe Christians are right,
but they are not close,
they only acknowledge the existence of God.

The Big Picture

God allows chaos in the midst of peace,
and
peace in the midst of chaos,

thus harmony is preserved.

Layers of Life

The many views of life,
come from the subtleties,
shadow upon shadow,
light upon light,
for a brief moment,
I catch you in the window of shadows past.

I Know You

I know you,
your face,

your glasses,
I will never forget,

the place,
the time,
the moment,

the memory?

the memory,
is lost!

lost in,
the time,
the place,
the moment,

yet, I know you,

your face,

your glasses,

I know you.

Contrasting The Blue Moon

There is no blue in a Blue Moon,

no blue in the Blues,
only life,

no one gets blue any more,
just depressed,

"blue skies are cloudy and grey",

Van Gogh got over his blue,
period!

there is no blue in a Blue Moon.

The World is Getting Old

I have your portrait Dorian,
but somehow, I think my mirror is broken,

I look into it and see cracks,
lines and creases,

must be some kind of flaw in the glass!

perhaps, the full length mirror in the parlor,
is starting to lose its clarity over time,

maybe, I should consider replacing the clear bulb in the antique light fixture,

is it true that bad lighting can cause cataracts?

I've got your portrait Dorian,

if only I could remember,
where I put it.

My Cat

She hovers over her dish,
silent, staring, not uttering a word,

she remains silent,

the dish, true to its nature,
is only there to serve,

should I be feeling guilty?

am I responsible for either the taste or texture of cat food?

she hovers over her dish,
silent, staring, not uttering a word.

What Would You Say to God

Is the gentle wind that blows across my thinning hair,
your way of telling me to enjoy the moment,
not to look back over my shoulder, nor to anticipate the
horizon, just to be present in the here and now?

are tears meant to be the lubricant of the soul, designed to
make the bodies of old and young alike, dance in unfettered
exuberance in times of great joy,
or in times of great sorrow and grief, are they likewise
meant to purge raging rivers of pain from our moments of
desperation and befuddlement?

is the night, void of light-a place of mystery and shadows,
meant to be a metaphor for our journey through this life,
are we solely responsible for searching and finding the
switch that will illuminate our path along this journey?

is the day, in its stunning brilliance and eye catching fancies,
merely a clever parlor trick-an illusion, meant to invite the
uninitiated to look beyond the curtain?

Why do you make us think?

In front of me are all the things that I know,

God, are you ultimately and solely, all the things that I
don't know?

Paradox Betrayal

At opposite ends of the earth,
people stand, feet firmly planted on the ground,

at the same moment,

whether, at the top or the bottom,
up is up to both and down is down,

silent thoughts occur,
both silent and heard at the same time,
the mind is listening,

a glass is empty,
yet at the same time filled by the space inside,

to live one must die,
the act of living,
and every breath thereafter,
steers one closer, ever closer to death,

is paradox to be considered one of nature's true mysteries,
a God like power?
allowing the inner-self to look outward at the same instant
that the outer-self looks inward,

is paradox a subversive force, responsible for setting the
stage for the epic battle between deductive and inductive logic,

does paradox dictate the rules that determine that all
answers must have a question,
conversely, that all questions must ultimately have an answer,

was paradox present when anthropologists discovered that
all human beings evolved from a single source in Africa,

or was that irony?

if so, does that mean that I am you and you are me,

if that's true, who tricked us into hating ourselves?

it's not man's inhumanity to man that we should be
concerned about but "my inhumanity to me!"

maybe Pogo was right.

Tapping on Cobblestones

The stones, much older than I,

stiff, unable to move,

aging in place,

standing firm,

stoic,

defiant to the ravages of time,

defined by their place in history,

not by the history of this place,

my cane, unwanted, not unexpected,

a relentless tapping on their heads,

a tapping born to awaken past memories,

a tapping,

no longer the familiar sounds of wagon wheels clanking,

the sound of shepherded sheep passing,

just an infernal tap, tap, tapping,

do the stones whisper?

do they recognize the light steppers from the heavy footed?

do they know when I'm coming?

"damn stones, stumbling beneath my feet"

why don't they get out of my way!

stop spoiling my vacation,

if it wasn't for those stones,

I could probably throw my cane away,

stop wasting my hard-earned money,

traveling the world,

chasing ancient history,

those darn stones are everywhere,

trying to make me fall,

hell I'm not the Holy Roman Empire!

just an old man with a cane,

tap, tap, tapping on their heads.

Cutting Firewood

I miss cutting firewood,

cutting, splitting, carrying, stacking,

scrounging kindling from the shake mill,

I miss the fitful hum of the chainsaw,

the Zen-like arrangement of the wood pile,

an ax swung with the intensity of John Henry's hammer,

splitting round after round,

splinters flying like sparks from a crackling fire,

the rude awakening of misguided swings,

sends jarring pain across the shoulders and through the spine,

now at age 75, a mindless flick of the remote turns on the gas fireplace,

when the remote's battery dies,

get into the car,

drive 5 miles,

spend 15 minutes to park,

spend 8 minutes to locate the battery section in the store,

spend 10 minutes in the checkout line,

5 to 6 minutes to find the car,

6 to 8 minutes to exit the parking lot,

5 miles back home,

at age 75, I miss cutting firewood.

Living on the Edge

The light of day,

a shadowed existence,

people moving,

a filtered image,

a scene strobed across a flashing background,

an Ansell Adams portrait,

people reaching out through the vulgar smoke-filled emptiness
to touch the outside world,

an epic tug of war between choice and circumstance,

they are a permanent fixture up and down the corridor,

Evergreen, I-99, to Aurora,

we have names for them,

they have names for us,

they see us,

we pretend to see them,

parasitic curiosities addicted to survival!

their world is not different from ours

only separate,

our society has never been without them,

they have never been without us,

neglected,

thrown out,

left out,

the outcome is the same!

they receive society's touch,
never its embrace,

either by choice or circumstance,

they prefer to live on the edge,
rather than with us,

makes one wonder,

"what do they know that we don't "?

City Of Ascending Spires (Seattle)

A city of ascending spires reaching past expectations,

soon to look mountain tops eye to eye,

precarious cranes dangling overhead,

raising the skyscape to new heights,

while Bertha works unseen in the depths,

to sew together the patchwork of progress.

Fragments and Phrases

There wasn't one in that pile of wood,
insulting phrase from the past didn't make me
smile,

wall-to-wall pile,
a 1960's carpet style,
wall falling in Berlin,
east to west,

Irving Berlin's White Christmas,
the Gettysburg Address,
shuffling feet,
blaring horns,
the noise of the city,
a crown of thorns,

hopscotch on the sidewalk,
single malt,
aged smokey peat,

a smooth Jazz phrase,
a funky downbeat,

foggy day in London Town,
head in the sky,
feet on the ground,

a taunt to juxtaposition,
beyond the poet's reach,
fragments and phrases,
a musical note, to soothe the savage beast,

Dexter Gordon

Life is all about
singing and dancing

Dexter Gordon whispers gently,
his saxophone sings,
as if prompted to remember lines

Matadors live,
because they dance

Running Backs escape,
for the same reason

Politicians dance

Dancers never step on toes,
Singers never go hungry

Jesus danced on water,
The Buddha on paradox,
someone sang for their supper

at 67 the dancing stopped,
the notes became airy,
the crowds sparse.

Perhaps

As time ages,
I can no longer put a face with a memory,

high school is a place frozen in time,
undaunted by successive reunions,
Viet Nam,
broken marriages,
climbs up the corporate ladder,

summer nights,
spent on the corner,
talking in the neutral zone,
are not taxable,

journeys planned,
remain,
between the covers of travel brochures,

memories of songs,
have outlived the singers,

time spent writing about life,
could be best spent,
living,

perhaps.

Comfort

Life is a tender twist,

from raised voices,
to teared eyes,

the structured web,
snags the spirit,

the wind offers,
no hand hold,

the stars, vessels of dreams,
sink beneath the weight of ambition,

the earth eats its children.

Gazing at the Cascades

The jagged fingers of the mountains,
poised to poke the stars in their eyes,
elicit tears to water the earth,

fulfill parched dreams,
of stargazing fools like me,

wandering moments of inattention,
punctuate the stop and go traffic of life,

the blaring horns of the freeway pulse,
harmonizes with the rhythmic honks,
of geese flying overhead,

the crest of the hill,
momentarily,
interrupts the monotonous moans,
of the marauding hordes,

life is but a mobius band,
challenging blind men,
to dance on its edges.

Stagnation

Living in a no man's land,

there is fullness in the void,

thoughts of stone men,

crest on the tears,

of time worn gods.

A Courtyard View of Spring

The distant hum of a vintage airplane stands in opposition to the harmony of late spring solace,

between the slotted spaces of a time-worn fence, variegated leaves on shrubs,

bathe in filtered sunlight,

perched like a curious child,

cabbage-sized crimson rhododendrons,

peek over the neighbor's fence,

a singing bird makes me smile,

a Hinoke stands alone having shaken off the yellow needles of winter's chill,

behind the shaded deep green corridor of trees,

unseen voices wage a battle of wills,

parent to child, child to parent,

in the street the familiar melody of the ice cream man rings out,

a siren call,

a call to arms,

memories from my youth,

time turned a dollar from a dime,

the mis-stepped sounds,

desperation!

tapping cane too slow to catch up with the trailing melody,

growing ever faint in the distance,

I struggle, like life,

images glide by,

unable to catch up with the Ice Cream Man,

unable to catch up with time,

I have become more, an observer than a participant,

stars rise, exploding like champagne bubbles,

contrails, of aircraft, passing overhead whitewash the night sky,

distant traffic on the highway rumble pass,

disturbing the whispered silence of a spring night.

Electra

The fragrant lights of ambrosia,

vacuolate the ethers,

the womb, advanced in the cycle,

arose to greet the dawn,

bliss prevailed,

thus the morning was called Electra,

Who Claims This Child?

I!

the rumblings, though subtle at first,

grew in intensity,

the sphere, throughout eternity,

had remained impervious to all forces, save one,

The Bearer of Will turned to face the intruder,

the incarnate wave surged forth,

shattering the womb,

laying bare the infant,

the carrion claw seized the spheres of consciousness,

each falling in endless array past the gaze of Shiva,

thus was illusion born,

time became a dimension,

the cosmic matriarch, Ohm,

meditated upon the silence,

the light held within each fragment, began to pulsate,

a gentle compelling force drew them homeward,

in its course, each search became a journey,

the vibrations of all levels brought forth new wisdom,

each in its own time,

came and stood in place around the compassionate matriarch,

with one mighty inhalation,

each was drawn into its place of being,

the dream ceased,

the infant slumbered in the womb,

Behold!

the morning was called Electra.

About the Author

Previously published in the *Arizona Centennial Anthology* and in five editions of *Between the Lines*, he is a board member for EPIC Group Writers, and chairs a monthly poetry group. He is the editor and a contributor to a recently published poetry anthology entitled, *Soundings from the Salish Sea (A Pacific Northwest Poetry Anthology)*.

He was selected to read his poetry at an event featuring Claudia Castro Luna, Washington State Poet Laureate. In 2019, he helped establish a bi-monthly *Poet's Corner* featurette in *My Edmonds News* to showcase the work of local poets.